Loving The Alcoholic In Your Life

Changing Your Behavior to Positively Change the Alcoholics Behavior

Antoinette Kinsmen

Table Of Contents

Chapter One: The Plan

You have probably been down this road many times. Your loved one begins drinking to the point of no return once again. A fight ensues, words are exchanged and it is another miserable episode of nagging and pleading and promises to refrain from ever returning to this point. Does this sound familiar? If this is the picture that represents your life, then it is time to enact an alternative to the repeated efforts of trying to make him or her quit this behavior.

This alternative is rather straightforward and does not require massive study to master these necessary tools. Instead, this is your opportunity to maneuver through the program and determine the choices you desire to make and what outcome you would like to see achieved. The pace at which you travel through the program is at your discretion. If you do not feel like putting in some effort, then you can almost be sure that this same negative path will continue as it has in the past. Conversely, if you give the alternative a go, there is a strong chance that it will improve.

The alternative being referred to is a vastly different approach to demanding and complaining. This entails an easy behavioral system with two goals and one main procedure. Those goals are to increase your quality of life and secondly, make a sober lifestyle look appealing to your loved one. This main procedure involves something by the name of "behavioral mapping". The central concept is to determine how the individual that drinks affects you and how to modify those patterns to achieve alternate results. What if it were possible to alter your reaction to your loved one's drinking? Thus, by doing so, you made it a more positive experience to skip the drinking altogether? That being said, the final outcome could be no drink, no complaining, no ensuing arguments and the quality of life could be far greater. In addition, your loved one could take a step towards a sober life.

That possibility may sound rather easy, or maybe you are one that looks at that idea and believes it is not probable. In all actuality it is easy *and* hard. While the techniques are simple to learn, it is the integration into your life that can be difficult. The method in which you and your loved one interact is similar to a well-rehearsed play. It has probably become second nature to you and your loved one, plus with the addition of alcohol impacting the behavior and brain of your drinker and the interaction of all that was previously mentioned makes any change a challenge.

In addition, the reality of your life is that there are crises that arise and are typically unexpected, habits that are difficult to break and an overall sense of discouragement that will require you to rise above it all. With that being said, just as you would not throw your hands up on a journey you ultimately desire simply because you have encountered some hurdles, you also will not throw your hands up on the possibility of altering your life with the alcoholic only because it is difficult. The only constant in life is change, and positive change requires some effort. In the end, the effort you put forth will be worth the effort you invested.

The Future

As we discussed, there are two simple goals when enacting this program. The first is to enhance your quality of life. What this equates to is not only getting your loved one to refrain from drinking, but to reinstate sanity back into your own life whether your loved one (dealing with alcoholism) is successful with giving up drinking, or not. That is the most important factor in this equation. (For our purposes, the individual that is drinking will be referred to as the drinker or loved one.)

Your life needs to stop being a roller coaster of ups and downs that are contingent upon your loved one being sober or drunk, happy or angry, out and about or at home. We will also discuss safety plans focused on keeping you from becoming a victim of violent behavior regardless of the mood of your drinker.

Moreover, the goal of bringing your loved one towards a sober life is also aided by increasing the quality of your life, regardless of his or her behavior. It is found that when your stress levels are lowered, you will have an improved ability to deal with your loved one in a more peaceful, less reactive mode, and the ultimate outcome can be an enhanced relationship. Thus, this will motivate your drinker towards a life without the alcohol.

Furthermore, the second goal is to make a sober lifestyle look more appealing. The unfortunate fact is that your improved outlook (which is quite necessary) is not sufficient in the accomplishment of goal number two. Because of this, we have also included some helpful alternatives to the typical complaining and harassing. At the foundation of nearly every strategy is the aforementioned "behavioral mapping".

As you move towards making these important changes, remember that change is a process, and often a slow process. Do not get discouraged but rather expect this journey. Those improvements that you desire will take time, but they are best achieved with careful consideration and adequate planning. Keep in mind how much time has passed where you have been handling your drinker in his or her current state. Remember how long you have lived with these set of drinking circumstances, thus you will be able to carry this burden a little longer as you enact these minute, controllable modifications. The crucial parts of these alternatives are the small steps which eventually can give way to big changes. As those changes take place and feel natural, you have a green light to add more. The information contained herein is yours to keep and work through at your pace.

What Lies Ahead

We have not even scratched the surface, but one can imagine the toil and stress you have already experienced. You are, more than likely, quite anxious to get started. Try this activity to get things moving. Take a blank sheet of paper and write down the details of your most recent altercation regarding the alcohol. What was said by both parties? What was stated and who did the speaking, first, next and so forth? You want to include so much detail that it appears just like a play script. Attempt to really digest everything. Then reflect on the given scenario such as drinker once again arrived late, set off spouse and an argument ensued. The course of the outcome for an argument could be different simply by altering how the spouse acts in response to the situation. For instance, one response by the non-drinker could have been anger at the prospect the drinker arrived late. The spouse could have then played the ignore game with little bits of underhanded coercion and complaining. A completely different response could have been alerting the drinker that the spouse did not enjoy when the drinker come home late after a drinking episode. The spouse could have added that while he or she loves the drinker, he/she has made other plans but dinner is ready. In this latter response, the drinker does not have an opportunity to become aggravated and drink. An argument does not have a chance to come into fruition and ultimately, the drinker knows he or she is loved but has to spend the remainder of the evening alone eating his or her dinner in solitude.

The Basis of the Program

This alternatives program is based on the principle that those most influential to the drinker are typically most important in the life of the drinker. It may be a negative reaction or a positive reaction, but nonetheless, the drinker has the greatest response to that close circle of influence. As an individual in that circle, you have the ability to direct those reactions in the most positive of directions.

In addition, you know your loved one very well, perhaps even better than he or she knows him/herself. Because you are motivated and determined to reach the goal of sobriety, you certainly hold power to navigate those changes.

Outcome Expectations

While other methods tend to endorse detachment from the drinker, that is not the case here. The underlying element is a push to make the relationship successful. The ingredients of empowerment, instruction and desire are our focal points. You will learn the necessary skills required to empower your own life and improve the relationship you have with your loved one. In addition to that, should your drinker choose to remain on the same path, you will have learned how to enhance your own life. If that latter scenario becomes your reality, you will feel at ease in releasing yourself from their life and you will have a clear conscience in doing so.

Chapter Two: Determining the Course

The basis of this chapter will be three main goals. Your first objective will be to ascertain a real consistency in the drinking patterns of your loved one. That information will then allow you to gain a clear "baseline", specifically the amount of drinking that is happening and the circumstances which surround that drinking. The final objective will be to take that information and devise an action plan that is both workable for changing your behavior and the behavior of the drinker.

Because you have gone through so many experiences with the drinker, it has almost become so second-natured that you can predict the next move. You might have even thought to yourself (or said out loud), 'It never fails. He always does this.' Look at this privileged information as your leg up. You have the unique ability to coerce the behavior of your drinker into the direction you choose. The first requirement will be to make a behavioral road map. In your experience with the drinker, for instance, determine what triggers your loved one to drink, what spikes and lowers the drinking, where do you belong in all of this?

This road map is comprised of three parts with the first being drinking triggers. Similar to a highway road sign, this tells you when the next exit is approaching. The next component is your loved one's initial signs that they are intoxicated. This would be akin to road showing signage for lowering your speed. While some signs are quite obvious, other ones are less noticeable and thus, that is when your judgment call will be necessary. For instance, your loved one may be in an irritated mood and you will need to determine whether that is due to perhaps something that happened at work, or on the ride home, or if a drink of alcohol is more consistent with this foul mood. The bottom line is whether your loved one is still on the road to sobriety. The final components to the map are any consequences due to drinking.

Moreover, let's say that your loved one does decide to take a drink. From there, several subsequent roads, or options, are presented to your drinker. Sometimes, your reaction can be the very thing that turns your drinker back to drinking. It is for this reason that trigger and sign identification are imperative to figure out the outcome that occurs between you and the drinker, when he or she drinks. The more you are informed about what specifically leads your loved one to drink and conversely, what leads him or her to sobriety will create positives for all.

Road Map: Things Which Prompt Drinking

Drinking triggers can be caused by a number of factors including, but not limited to, moods, individuals, events, days, aromas, times or even thoughts. In addition, they can serve as the catalyst to want a drink or to actually drink. Each individual may have their own unique trigger; however, some factors seem to be rather common for many. Please read this list and see what possibly rings true for your situation.

- Speaks of life's hopelessness
- Unhappiness at work
- Children are loud (in the eyes of the drinker)
- Woman's menstrual cycle or PMS (Premenstrual Syndrome)
- Nothing better to do
- Great day at work
- Going to work at all
- Schedule is too busy
- Viewing sports by themselves
- Feelings of depression
- High on life and the urge to party
- A simple reason to bring on an argument
- Complaints regarding a boss or co-worker
- Friends are coming over
- Riding home with coworkers or friends

Perhaps there are some other triggers that are consistent with your drinker that we might have missed. Go ahead and add those triggers to the list and then give a summarization which reflects the typical pattern displayed by your loved one.

Sally's Typical Drinking Pattern

Sally works as a trauma nurse and frequently experiences high stress situations. In addition to her occupation, she is also *like* a single mother to two young boys (as her husband is a military pilot and is often away from home). Sally also cares for an elderly parent, her mother. There are often times when Sally expresses frustration at the small size of her house, her skyrocketing bills with daycare and other expenses and the lack of time for herself.

In reading this aforementioned scenario, Sally often participated in drinking when the beginning of the month came around and a plethora of bills arrived. Her other triggers were during stressful moments of uncertainty over her mother's health and her frequent trips to the E.R. or when she returned home after a horrendous day at work with trauma to a child. She could not handle the sight of children going through torment.

While drinking does not always follow a 'trigger', you can usually see a pattern forming. Often times, this pattern precedes an episode of heavy drinking.

Road Map: Drinking's Warning Signs

You might feel more established in what causes your loved one to grab a drink, but now it is important to figure out what signs he or she exhibits that signifies your loved one has already been drinking. In between that first taste of alcohol to the point of drunkenness, those drinking signs are usually posted to inform you that your loved one has moved from a place of sobriety into a state of drunkenness. From the moment alcohol reaches the brain, the individual will have difficulty being able to think with a clear mind. When this point is reached, your first objective needs to be safety. If violence is ever resorted to by your drinker then you need to execute a safety plan. (We will be discussing that in one of the further chapters.) If safety is not a concern, then the second objective needs to become your primary focus – do not encourage any further drinking by any of your actions. The behavioral maps that you are working to develop will assist you in successfully reaching this goal.

Look at these common drinking signs and determine which rings true for your situation. At the beginning of each sign, recite 'I know he or she (loved one) has been drinking when…

- Wants solitude
- Is highly emotional
- Does not want to eat
- Goes to the store to purchase a case, several bottles or some hard liquor
- Speech is difficult to understand or is slurred
- Eyes appear glassy
- Violent mood swings
- Family withdrawal
- Fists or jaws are tight and clenched
- Eyelids are droopy
- Paces
- Is less emotional
- Speaks in a loud tone or more quiet tone of voice
- Justifies drinking because of job, stress or life in general and states that he or she deserves at least one drink

You might not see drinking signs that are consistent with your loved one. Feel free to add those to your map so you can paint the most detailed picture. Part one and two are now completed.

Road Map: Costs Arising From Drinking

This final component to the map involves identification of steps which ultimately leads to drinking-related issues or general drinking. Once this is determined then you will have an easier time figuring out how to alter that pattern.

Take a quiet moment and review memory lane. What resulted because of your loved one's drinking? Without this vital information, your map will not be complete. Some of those consequences may not have occurred right away while others may have been brought on immediately. As peculiar as it may sound, also determine any positive outcomes that resulted from your loved one drinking. Perhaps their drinking ensured their dependency upon you or they were happier drunk. Knowing those positives from drinking will soften some of the blow when those sober changes start taking place. Please read these consequences and see if they apply to your loved one after drinking.

- Absent from work
- Becomes fatigued or sick
- Emotions of shame or guilt
- Partakes in reckless or unsafe behavior
- Becomes the life of the party
- Job loss
- Repressed sexual relationship
- Sexual relationship is less inhibited
- Trouble with law (DUI, DWI, car accident, arrested)
- Less interest in our relationship
- Lost employment/fired
- Trepidation of violence
- Experienced violence
- Inability to perform sexually
- Other issues are put on the back burner because drinking is always first issue
- Avoidance of a sexual relationship that is not satisfying
- Financial Issues
- Inability to let loose and relax
- Loved one's, or your property (or possessions), damaged
- Security in knowing loved one will always need me
- Physically becomes less attractive
- Drinking behavior is awkward and embarrassing
- Socially has a bad rap in the community
- Weight Issues
- Loss of friendships

Once again, you may have your own list of consequences that apply to your scenario. Ponder on those and add them to the list.

Determine a "Baseline" for your drinker. This will serve as your starting point. To ascertain the amount your loved one is drinking, you will want to describe his or her current drinking trends. The underlying reason this is so important is to finalize the map with all the necessary information and for the purposes of progress recognition as you see fit.

The next step is to determine the amount and the regularity with which your loved one drinks. For instance, what did yesterday look like? Considering the day before, how much drinking took place? Does your loved one tend to drink more or less during the week? How about the weekend? In order to gain a better picture, you may want to consult a calendar. You can use the following as a guideline as each item counts as one drink:
- Wine – 14 oz.
- Beer – 12 oz.
- Liquor (80 Proof) – 1 ¼ oz.

- Liquor (100 Proof) – 1 oz.

The reason these amounts are established this way is due to their amount of ethanol. Ethanol is the chemical found in alcohol which is responsible for making it a drug. Each of the aforementioned amounts contains ½ ounce of ethanol.

Usual Weekly Drinking Patterns

1.) Estimate the number of drinks consumed during a typical Monday, Tuesday, Wednesday and Thursday. You will then want to multiply that usual intake daily amount by four. _____
2.) Estimate the number of drinks consumed during a routine Friday. _____
3.) Estimate the number of drinks consumed during a routine Saturday. _____
4.) Estimate the number of drinks consumed during a routine Sunday. _____
5.) Figure the total of questions 1 through 4. _____

You will want to keep in mind that not all individuals have Friday through Sunday as their typical weekend. Some work schedules vary so you will need to adjust accordingly. In addition, keep in mind that certain vacations or special events might cause your loved one to drink more. This will want to be a part of your configuration.

Furthermore, as a part of your costs and drinking pattern, you will want to include those times spent at the bar, the liquor store and other alcohol-related activities. How much time did your loved one deal with a hangover? Did he or she ever end up going to jail? Did he or she ever go to the hospital due to alcohol? This in-depth look of where your loved one is today will give you a better picture of where you want to ultimately end up tomorrow.

Often times, drinking will cause you many a needless argument. Perhaps others can handle more alcohol than your loved one or there are other times you feel as though you are just involved in battle after battle and you start to wonder if all these battles are really worth the effort? After all, is my loved one drinking normal? Almost assuredly, if you questioned several individuals that drink then you might receive several definitions to that answer. It is for this reason that we can simplify to a bottom line answer: If the amount of alcohol being consumed is causing issues, then clearly that is too much alcohol.

In addition, try to stray from ever calling someone an alcoholic. Leave this label to the experts. There have been many individuals that have gone the opposite direction from treatment due to this stigmatized label. In the end, labeling your loved one is not really necessary or helpful.

Make a New Reconfigured Map

When you attempt to reconfigure the map, you will want to reconsider the way in which you handle your loved one to minimize or lessen those triggers leading to drinking. Thus, instead of watching the drinker going from one scenario of drinking to the next, you can transition positively to creating new roads that takes those old drinking triggers into new activities that are non-drinking. Let's take a look at this example:

John and Beth

Beth was a stay-at-home mother of three children. John worked as an accountant at a prestigious company and made enough of a sizeable income that Beth could focus on her children and take some classes for her real estate license. While the children were at school, Beth would clean and run errands and then focus on preparing for her upcoming exam. John had only worked at this new company for six months. Even though John's income was a welcome sight, the stress and his increased drinking every Friday and Saturday were also causing Beth considerable stress. She lived for Monday through Thursday because the post-effects of John's drinking were miserable. The children were also negatively affected. They refused to bring friends over on the weekend and were become more and more distant from their father. Beth was highly concerned about this and decided to map out John's drinking. She included new behaviors that she could enact in order to elicit alternative behaviors from John. When Friday approached, she decided to make one of John's favorite dishes, her famous pizza. The aroma of pizza wafted through their home and was an inviting smell from the moment he walked through the door. Instead of giving him an opportunity to grab a drink, she took his briefcase and sat him down to give him a neck and shoulder massage. As he sat, tired and yet anxious from the day's events, he sat quietly until he decided to tell Beth about his day. Typically, the week's events would have caused John to want a beer, but having the opportunity to feel appreciated and loved (via the back rub and offering her listening ear), he started refraining from those Friday night drinks. By Saturday morning, John was more chipper and relaxed and not reeling from the night of drinking. John was able to be an active parent and the children started to enjoy their father. The greater the number of positive experiences, the more John was able to shift his thinking away from drinking and towards life's pleasantries.

As you can see by Beth's behavior, she re-mapped her husband's (John) drinking behavior. In order to apply this to your life, pick the top two or three most common triggers found in your loved one. For each one that is chosen, take the time to really ponder and give great detail. Ask the W questions for each trigger like when, where, why and so forth and do not forget to add the consequences.

For the above story example, it might look something like this:
John comes home on Friday and is full of tension -> Beth tells John about her tiresome day -> John proceeds to the liquor cabinet and pours himself a highball -> Beth notices what John is doing and questions whether John is going to make this another drunken Friday -> John rolls his eyes and states 'Here we go again!' -> Beth pleads for John to calm down and think of the kids -> John yells at Beth that all he does is work for her and the kids and why can't he just kick back with a relaxing drink -> Beth retreats to her office -> John finishes off one drink and pours another -> Beth comes back in to try and calm the situation down -> She sees John polishing off another drink and he looks like he is becoming visibly drunk -> Beth is crying and John is reticent

Study the map and look for the areas with the most issues or the most common triggers. Is it possible this trigger is happening because of something deeper? For instance, John's unhappiness at work is out of Beth's hands. But let's pretend that John has a strong trigger to hit a bar that is on his way home from work. Maybe, on Friday's Beth could offer to meet him at his favorite pizza restaurant. In this way, the Friday night drinking binge could be avoided and replaced with a fun and happier alternative.

Moreover, if Beth (for example) were to be greeted by typical Friday drinking John where he almost assuredly will work on becoming plastered, then Beth has the choice to follow the old road map. She can tell John how upset he is making her and how disappointed she is in him, then John will grow aggravated and drink into an oblivion and the day will end in a turbulent mess. On the other hand, the choice is there to create a new map and improve your chances of a happy ending.

Chapter Three: Violence is Not Welcome

Violence is often a part of drinking alcohol. As we know, alcohol can make a person do various things. It can also turn an even-temper into rage. The key element in working to alter the behavioral map is to ensure your safety and the safety of those around you. Even if you have not witnessed a verbal or physical violence in your drinker, you will still want to take in this information just for the sake of preparation.

If violence is a possible issue that you and your loved one have struggled with, then you will want to be cautious. You will want to make any adjustments with careful consideration simply because the risk of violence is possible. You may even want to consult with a mental health professional if you are able. There may be some uncertainty as to what violence is. This quiz, found below, will help you to determine whether or not violence is an issue.

Violence Quiz

1.) Your loved one arrives at the bowling league practice and has a stench of alcohol on his or her breath. When you merely question the drinker, he or she becomes irate and pushes you away with some aggression.
2.) Your loved one arrives late to the parent teacher conference and you question him/her as to where he/she has been. He/she goes into a tirade of swearing and name calling and threats.
3.) While in the midst of a heated debate, you are interrupted by a neighbor noticing that you are outside. Out of concern, the neighbor tries to calm the situation by talking sense to the drinker. The drinker then turns and makes the neighbor feel about two inches tall after laying into him/her. The yelling, screaming and flailing arms can be seen by anyone.
4.) You just discovered that your young child that you are trying to potty train has just soiled his pants. In the midst of hurriedly trying to clean the child you see that your loved one has just noticed the child's mess in his pants. Without further thought, your loved one flies into a fit of rage and spanks your little boy with such force, you are sure your drinker has even hurt his/her spanking hand.
5.) You and your spouse are out to dinner and your wife has thrown back another glass of wine. She is clearly not in her correct frame of mind and is starting to make a scene over the food. She asks the waiter to come over and orders him to remake her fillet mignon as it is too overcooked. As she aggressively orders the waiter to make it right or else, you try to calm her down so she will not make a scene. She fires back at you and tells you to shut your face or else you will be sorry for embarrassing her.
6.) You receive a call from your wife that she needs to be picked up from a girl get together happy hour. When you arrive, her speech is far worse than even on the phone call. You gently grab her hand to encourage her to the car and she aggressively pulls away and spits on you and then storms out.

If any of those above scenarios would be labeled non-violent by you then you will really want to reconsider how you view violence. According to the dictionary there are approximately four different definitions for violence and they stem from pushing and hitting to taking the words you say and negatively manipulating them, swearing or profanity, hurling of objects and threats. Each scenario listed above involves violence.

Escape Plan

In the midst of violence it is imperative to enact some plan for safety. This works best when it is already thought of and prepared in advance. Your first objective will be to have a small emergency suitcase with two to three days of belongings. In addition, you would want to include a bag for each child just in case you need to make a quick exit.

Once the suitcase has been packed, you can keep it safe at a safe house or in the trunk of your car. The definition of a safe house is any place where your drinker would not be allowed access to you. Be mindful of your children (if you have any) when considering a location for a safe house. In addition, it would be best to have several safe houses lined up for availability of one house if another is unavailable or if your drinker has forced their way into one of the safe houses.

Similar to the way heat builds up when water is put on the stove; there are also similar signs that often precede violence. These are typically termed, 'red flags'. Some possible examples of red flags might be an angered stare, jaw protrusion, even verbal signs that the individual is shutting down and on the verge of becoming irate.

When you can see or sense that red flags are happening, you need to remind yourself that proving a point is not worth the aggression that follows. Your safety and the safety of your children (if you have children) is the first priority. If you desire to spend more hours of the day in a non-drinking environment with your loved one, or be influential in the number of drinks consumed, then you may find exercising a little restraint at the beginning will have larger payoffs for you in the future.

As you and your drinker are becoming heated, several things happen. The hostility and anger that spills out from your drinker also causes you to become more and more angered. It becomes a double-edged sword of identifying those red flags and bringing your own emotions to a controlled level. When this is executed properly, you are able to respond in a safe manner.

When the War is Already Started

Let's imagine that you and your drinker have already become embattled. The red flags have come and gone and now you are faced at the receiving end of the outburst of rage. Take this opportunity to end the violence to regain safety. After all, your physically harmed body will not assist you in making your point in the argument.

If the argument has escalated, leave the premises and get yourself out into the public open space. This will allow others to see what is happening and offers them an opportunity to help you if you need it or to remove the children (if any are there) from the scene. These individuals can also serve as witnesses to the violence if the need ever arises.

The police are also at the end of three digits – call 911. Perhaps this has happened before and you placed 911 on your speed dial. Regardless of whether you are able to remain on the line after phoning 911 or not, the police station will be able to trace you to your address from a landline phone. Help will be on its way.

The most important thing is to calm the situation. No individuals should get hurt or injured, thus if the aggressor demands an apology or money then respond to those demands by giving what is ordered. You can always back track later when you are out of harms way, but in the midst of an altercation, safety is your number one priority.

Chapter Four: Where Do You See Your Future?

Think about your life and where it is going. Where would you like it to go? Your best life would look like, what? Think about this in detail and then come back later with any new thoughts. Here is an exercise which might jog some of those details.

1.) Think about your life in the past and consider any activities that used to be enjoyable to you and your drinker that you no longer participate in. Give your top three activities?

2.) Think about your current situation and the behaviors and activities of your drinker. What would you like to see removed from that bright future picture?

3.) Think of those positive activities your drinker currently engages in that you find appealing. What activities would you like to see happening more often?

4.) Think of your bucket list (those things you would like to accomplish or do before your leave this earth). What activities on your shared bucket list would you like to do with your drinker?

Hopefully, you have taken the time to give great detail to the above exercise. Too often individuals will just give a blanket statement of what they want and the detail is lacking. Some example blanket statements would include, 'I just want to get along with my spouse.' Another statement might be, 'I yearn for happiness in my life.' What do these statements really look like to you? This is where your custom details are so imperative to the success of these statements. You want to be able to feel it, see it and touch it with those details. It is with those clear goals that you are able to move towards reaching them.

Furthermore, those goals need to become concrete goals and not merely unsubstantial wishes. Your behavioral map will need clear directions. For instance, the line stating that you want to help your drinker to get on the road to sobriety involves various goals. For some, help could mean varying your behavior to push your drinker towards less drinking. Help could also mean removing yourself entirely to stop enabling your drinker and force him/her to make good decisions themselves.

In addition, sober can mean a variety of things. Proper management of drinking to the point of being able to refrain from intoxication or sensory impairment might be one individual's definition of sobriety. Another person may feel that completely removing alcohol from their life is the only true definition of sobriety. As you can see, a clear definition is imperative to success.

Here are some examples of goals with a clear statement:

1.) I will take the time to study and define the behavioral map for my loved one. Those strategies will serve as my guide for how I respond to his/her behavior and for what I desire for our lives together.

2.) I will make life more difficult for my loved one to drink. This includes my refraining from future cover ups and cleaning up of the messes he/she creates. These messes include both the physical and the mental.

3.) I will activate my calming mechanisms and mentally repeat the words 'red flag' when I see an argument escalating to uncomfortable levels. My life and the lives of my children and the drinker are more important to me than always being right.

In the midst of all this behavior manipulation and behavioral mapping, you may feel that you are quickly becoming overwhelmed. It is important that you give yourself some breathing room and time to relax. It is never easy making hard decisions and you should be commended for the effort you are putting forth. Think of the steps that have already been taken and your proactive voyage to bring positive changes to your life and the lives of those you love. You deserve credit for all that you are doing. When the road becomes treacherous, remind yourself of the gift you are giving and the journey you have taken to arrive even at this destination. The final goal is an accumulation of several baby steps.

Chapter Five: Taking Control of the Situation

The long and hot days of summer were becoming a reality in the Smith home. With two children married and living on their own, the youngest was their only one left before the empty nest syndrome set in. Mrs. Smith was able to stay at home throughout her children's lives and she had enjoyed every minute of it. Her youngest son, Jerry, was saving up money by painting homes. He had become a part of an older crew and had befriended most of his co-workers. Because they were in their early twenties, many would enjoy a beer after work, but Jerry could not join them on their tailgates and after work get togethers, or so Mrs. Smith thought. She soon was noticing that Jerry was not acting as himself, was quick to anger and had even been involved in a brawl during the work hours that injured his shoulder. Jerry did not seem like his old self and she was starting to dread the hours he was at home. It soon became apparent that Jerry had been drinking with the guys and was finding he liked the alcohol and needed the alcohol. Alcohol was quickly becoming his new best friend...

Taking control of the situation involves two important things. The first is that you have the belief in yourself that you have the right to take control. The other component is that you have the belief that you can direct that control in the best possible direction.

Component One: Permission to Take Control

You may not believe or even understand, however sometimes it is essential that you care so much about those you love by first taking the measures to show yourself love first. If your emotions are revolving around fear, anger or hopelessness, you will not be able to effectively help the person that you love. Your calmness and ability to have clarity in thinking is contingent upon those aforementioned negative emotions not serving as a distraction. If your loved one is abusing alcohol, their clear thinking is highly impaired. If you focus all your energies on the drinker, then who is invested in caring for the relationship?

A common outcome of a drinker's alcohol abuse is that the drinker's problem strips others of their dignity and self-confidence. The drinker has lost, or is losing, their sense of control, so they will often look to those closest to them as their target for blame. Sometimes, this persistent tug at confidence will cause those that surround the drinker to actually blame themselves for the problem. When it reaches that point, the individual that is not secure in their own emotions will just add this to the seething pot and will ultimately lack the ability to help the situation entirely.

You need to stop the cycle and understand that you were not responsible for this person's abuse of alcohol. Stress is a real part of everyday life. Some cope with stress by finding healthier outlets and some cope by drinking. You are not to blame and the sooner you understand that the better. Because you are not to blame, so should you also not pay the debt for the problem. Thus, the sooner you stop this frustrating cycle and focus on your own health and happiness, the sooner you will have enough energy to participate in positive interaction with your drinker.

Remember You are Not to Blame

It becomes so easy to take the blame for the alcohol. When the drinker is your lover, you may not even feel the urge to have intimate relations anymore. Perhaps, the main emotion that you ever see coming from the drinker is that of pure anger.

It is during these difficult periods that you have to remind yourself that you did not desire for this to become the new life reality. You did not want your loved one to drink to such an extreme that he or she has now become so dependent upon alcohol. You did not choose this lifestyle and you are not to blame.

Let's go back to the scenario with Jerry and his mother. Take a look at these two varieties of reactions:

Option A: Jerry was laid off of work because his boss was tired of one too many call offs when he full well knew why Jerry missed work. He was hung over. Jerry's mother sees him slacking off and laying on the couch in old clothes. She tires of his lack of ambition and sees his life spiraling out of control so she forcefully awakens him at six in the morning and orders him to look for another job right then. As she awakens him she yells a slew of undesirable angered words and he quickly fires back calling her every name in the book. He slams the door and leaves.

Option B: Sleeping on the couch in his day old clothing, Jerry's mother bites her tongue and waits for Jerry to wake up. Eventually Jerry awakens and is reeling from his own discomforts of a hangover. After he has taken a shower, his mother approaches him and tells him that there are breakfast items in the refrigerator, but she needs to speak with him as the two eat together. Later that morning, the two sit together and the door is wide open for his mother to lay down what she will and will not accept.

These were two different reactions to the same situation. In the first situation, the emotions were far more fired up. Jerry's mother added the fuel to that fire and caused her son to put up even more of a guard. Her reaction triggered a more angered response from Jerry. The second situation was handled with greater influence coming from Jerry's mother. She was able to bring out Jerry's non-aggressive reaction by the way she handled the situation.

When you are in the midst of getting upset about future scenarios, it is imperative that you come from a place of thinking clearly and not clouded by emotion. The way in which you react can have a constructive, unconstructive or indifferent effect on the behavior of the drinker. The conversation should be conducted in a composed way that is non-confrontational but does not avoid the elephant in the room. In addition, you will be best received when you form your words in a positive way. An example of this would be, 'Honey, I appreciate it when you are on top of those clothes coming out of the dryer. It really helps me as I have wrinkle-free clothes to put in your closets.'

You have been given the tools to take control of the situation. How you operate with those tools will depend upon each individual. In addition to utilizing the tools, you need to feel that you harness the power to control the situation as well. Your loved one's drinking is not the responsibility of you and you are not to blame. We all make our own decisions in life. The way in which you respond and behave is your responsibility, thus the way you formulate your words and keep a cool clear head can have the capacity to make a positive difference in those interactions with your loved one.

Chapter Six: Bring On the Happiness

The title may seem out of place when discussing such a serious topic. Take a walk down memory lane and think of all those moments that were dedicated to you being there for your loved one. How many times did you place your needs onto the back burner to ensure the safety of your loved one (or your children) from your loved one's drinking? You need to pat yourself on the back for all the work you have invested. Ensure even yourself that all of your efforts have not fallen on your blind eyes. You are to be commended!

The way to accomplish this rewarding of self is to offer yourself a small bite of pleasure every single day. There are various forms that reward can be manifested. For instance, you can lift yourself with verbal expression. For instance, "I am proud of the perseverance I am giving to this family." Those are more simple gifts to self. The next classification requires some expense or thought. An example might be a guilt-free movie of your choosing or a visit to your favorite restaurant. It is something where you have to plan and extend yourself even more in the reward department. The final classification involves both planning and money. For instance, let's say you enjoy a full cleaning detail job on your vehicle. This will require planning and will cost money, but it will also fulfill a grandiose accomplishment like keeping a potential temper at bay when it was very difficult to avoid.

We will be giving more attention to creating that list of happiness, but first let's give some substance to determining that model for pleasure. For instance, one reward that was mentioned was a visit to your favorite restaurant. An activity such as this is typically enjoyed with your loved one. Prior to you proposing the idea with your loved one, you will need to think clearly as to what he/she will add to this reward. Can you count on this individual to be in sound mind and body for this meal? Will he or she embarrass you with your dinner turning into a night of drinking? You want to be mindful of turning a good reward into a bad punishment. Part of the process of healing is both the drinker and their partner entering into therapy to improve both of their lives together.

Conversely, the other side to the coin of reward is enjoying activities that are free of the influence of that substance (like alcohol). You will maximize the happiness you share together while minimizing the available time for drinking. Consequently, your loved one benefits, you benefit and your relationship flourishes.

Conjure Up Those Things that Make You Happy

Consider those things that bring you joy in life. Grab a sheet of paper and divide the paper into three sections so you can incorporate a rewarding system that coincides with the three previously discussed rewards. Remember the first column are for those rewards that are instant and do not involve a cost, the second column is less costly but requires some time and the final category involves both time and money.

Enlarge Your Social Circle

It is common to isolate and retract from others when they could serve to benefit and support you. They want to be there for you, but you have to enlarge your circle as opposed to closing them off. Consider those you feel closest to, whether they are family members, friends or even co-workers. Shorten your list by extracting any individuals that you do not enjoy their friendship or their influence on your life.

Moreover, as you engage with others, you may feel tenseness in entering those social circles. How will they receive you? Will it be awkward or will they wonder where you have been all of this time? Put yourself in their position and consider how you would feel. More than likely you would feel honored to get a call to get together. If the outcome is not as you had hoped, do not be downtrodden as this opportunity may not have worked out but possibly another future opportunity will present itself.

Every individual needs that one person with whom they feel they can trust and confide. Before finding that confidante, be sure to have clarity in the goals you are looking for. Sometimes a clear plan or goal with some invested time to think about what you desire will lead you to the right person. For instance, "I would like to find a friend that will simply be a sounding board to me and will not think less of me or my loved one. I need to be able to trust that what I say stays between him/her and me." Once that is clearly established, your next objective is to determine who fits the bill.

After you have considered the right person, then figure out how you would like to approach that individual. Once you determine that game plan, it is essential that you be direct with your questions. Let them know that you appreciate their friendship and that you trust them and then ask if they would be willing to go out sometime so you can talk. Be direct about needing their support and listening ear as you entrust them with some delicate topics in your life.

Sometimes, a little practice makes perfect. Try saying what you would say in front of a mirror or rehearse in the car. Wherever you go over your lines, focus on minimizing that insecurity and nervousness. When the time is right, go for it and ask for some support from that chosen friend. Bring on the happiness; it is time to have that important 'me' time.

Chapter Seven: Stop the Allowing Cycle

When you look at the life of the drinker and the life of their partner, it is common for the partner to become the responsibility portion of the relationship. Without the partner's vital role, things would tend to fall apart. Unfortunately, in fulfilling that position, two things take place with the first being your life can fall to pieces in an effort to substantiate the drinker. Your energy can be siphoned from you and your health suffers as a result. In the end, the ultimate price will be that regardless of the hard work you put out, it will become less effective over time.

The other outcome is that you lay the foundation or groundwork for their life without complication, thus life becomes easy for the drinker thanks to all of your efforts! Life may be crumbling and out of control, but as long as you maintain the position of fixer and cleaner, the drinker will be out of touch with reality and thus will remain on this path of destruction. In essence you are telling the drinker that you are fine with the drinking, even if the words that escape your mouth seem to be complaints and threats. Your actions speak so loudly that you cannot hear the words you are saying.

Let's look at the life of Robert and Elisha

Elisha was the 'It' girl at the office. Every guy had fun with her flirtatious style and fun character. It certainly did not hurt that she was beautiful. After several attempts, Robert finally swayed her to leave the single party girl life and become his girlfriend. Many of Robert's co-workers were jealous that Robert was able to seal the deal and have Elisha as his girlfriend. Life was an absolute thrill at first. They enjoyed each other's company, went on trips and were the envy of everyone at the office. The only negative part was that many of the fun times revolved around drinking. Robert would drink socially and limit himself, but Elisha had always loved alcohol and the way it made her express herself. Robert was quickly going from being upset and frustrated to holding deep-seated anger towards Elisha. Sometimes he had to nurse her back to health after a hangover or call in to make excuses as to why she would not be at work that day. Robert and Elisha were at odds and bickering constantly.

Elisha would apologize time and time again. Once her mental faculties were in place following an alcohol haze, she would take a stance to limit her drinking and plead for forgiveness from Robert. Each time she seemed so convincing and Robert had grown to love Elisha and wanted the best for her. When he called her boss at their workplace, he felt he was preventing her from being fired and having the difficulty of finding a new job. In addition, he loved the attention from the other guys at work and he led a life of lies by portraying a hot and sizzling life with Elisha.

Reading the story of Robert and Elisha you can see that Robert is frustrated and full of despair. His verbal expressions towards Elisha are to stop drinking, yet his more powerful silent message is that he is accepting her drinking and that he will be there to pick up the pieces that are a result of her drinking.

Think about your life and your interactions with your drinker. Were there times you called in to their boss to alleviate your loved one from the disappointment of being fired from a job? Did you ever make excuses for his/her behavior around friends? Did you ever lose a little piece of self-worth every time you silently picked up the pieces so rapidly falling apart at the hands of your drinker? Did you nurse your drinker as he/she was sick from drinking or practically comatose on the couch? Did you loan money to bail your loved one out from another jail stint that was a direct result of drinking?

There are far too many things to add to the list and you might have even thought of your own applicable enabling moments. By now, you and your loved one have interacted for some time in this manner and to veer off in another direction will be difficult even for you. That discomfort that you might feel is typical during the initial stages, regardless of those changes being positive. Sometimes, the urge to resist is felt for a multitude of reasons.

"If he changes, he might abandon me."

"I have come to terms that this is how Sally will always be."

"My mother has done so much for me throughout my life. Now it is my turn to look out for her regardless of how she lives now."

Remind yourself that the definition of insanity is repeatedly doing the same thing and expecting a different result. This dance is not working and your drinker will not be magically cured. The time is now to take on a new shield that is impenetrable against what your drinker or you may deal with in the face of change.

The best lessons learned are in those valleys. If your loved one is put in jail, let them learn that you will not be there to solve that problem. If your loved one has come home sloshed and becomes sick all over their clothes, let them bring resolve to the situation. If they are going to choose to make those decisions, they will soon learn during those difficult times that they never again, want to be in that situation.

Complaints, Loving and a Whole Slew of Emotions

There has inevitably come a time or two when you and your loved one have engaged in the battle of complaints. The complaining has been your action as a direct result of your drinker's actions. While you may feel that you are verbally posing a punishment to your loved one by letting them know how frustrated you are, you may unknowingly be tipping the balance of power in their direction. After all, this behavior continues regardless of your complaints, yet you are investing time and time again of your energy reserves. He or she is receiving your attention because you are giving it over and over via your complaints.

Moreover, you love your drinker and you want to keep him/her from harm. What you may see as innocent love and safeguarding could truly be hindering. If you always save them from harm, then they will not learn to protect themselves. You are that shield that is always there which allows them to never fall.

Perhaps you do not see the error of your ways in providing that safety net. Please read this list of times that called for your protection and mark it with a check if it is applicable to you. If you have done it more than one time in the past six months, then mark with the correct number of times you have done that action.

- Nursed your loved one back to health after an episode of drinking
- Called your loved one's work for the purpose of them not being present (due to drinking)
- Posted bail as a result of drinking
- Cleaned up a vomit mess
- Driven or picked up your loved one from a drinking establishment
- Made excuses to friends or family members that suspect your loved one is drinking too much
- Offered a night of home drinking by purchasing the liquor and making it available at home
- Refrained from any plans or get togethers due to your loved one's drinking
- Stayed up late to ensure your loved one arrived home and out of harm's way
- Served as the alarm clock for your loved one
- Smoothed over your loved one's drinking to prevent them from being down on themselves
- Minimized your life in any way from the amount of money you have spent on yourself, your children, time elements, etc. so your drinker's life would not be affected.

The time has come for you to visibly see what your drinker is doing to your life and the lives of those that surround him/her. There is a price that is being paid, but too often that price is not paid by the drinker, but rather by you. If you checked off even one thing then you can see a trend is forming. The drinker gets to enjoy the lifestyle because you will always be there. Is this starting to sound repetitive to you?

Now that you can see what is happening, take the time to see the actions that you do and decide to let go of those old habits. While they may die off like a Hollywood monster movie that keeps coming back to life, the more effort you put into permanently ending this cycle, the lower the chances of it continuing. Congratulations for coming this far, you are well on your way to positive changes for you and your loved one.

Chapter Eight: Final Thoughts

As you embark on this new journey understand that like any new thing it takes time. We have learned that studying the behavioral road map of your loved one can be instrumental in creating change. The efforts you exert in making that behavioral map customized to the struggles and issues you see fit will assist in becoming that much more applicable. You will have a map and compass for where you are and where you want to go.

We have also mentioned the strategies that have been tried and failed. Hopefully you see how many emotions are tied into the dance that you have shared with your loved one. They are learned responses and those behavioral paths have been tramped and trotted on for so long that the creation of a new path takes some effort. Unfortunately, your new methods may not be well-received by you or your loved one, but anything worthwhile is never easy. Keep at this.

The communication factor is crucial and the way in which words are formed requires a clear head and a heart which is strong enough to prevail for the better good, despite some of the bumps thrown your way. When your loved one sees that you are working together and that you hold enough love to want to make it better, the outcome has a greater chance of success.

Keep on that road and should you veer off, pick up this book and work to get your internal engine re-directed back onto the right path. Someday, you will thank yourself for doing this…

Made in the USA
Lexington, KY
22 April 2017